Read All About
Horses

WILD HORSES

LYNN M. STONE

The Rourke Corporation, Inc.
Vero Beach, Florida 32964

PHOTO CREDITS:
© James H. Robinson: cover, page 13; © William Munoz: pages 4, 9, 12, 18; © Lynn M. Stone: pages 6, 7, 10, 15, 16, 19, 21, 22

EDITORIAL SERVICES:
Penworthy Learning Systems

Library of Congress Cataloging-in-Publication Data

Stone, Lynn M.
    Wild horses / Lynn M. Stone.
        p. cm. — (Horses)
    Includes index.
    Summary: Describes the history and physical characteristics of the wild horses found in the western United States.
    ISBN 0-86593-513-0
    1. Wild horses—Juvenile literature. [1. Wild horses. 2. Horses.] I. Title
II. Series: Stone, Lynn M. Horse.
SF360.S76 1998
599.665'5—dc21   98–25096
                                                                    CIP
                                                                    AC

Printed in the USA

TABLE OF CONTENTS

Wild Horses 5

Wild Horse History 6

The Fall of Wild Horses 8

The Wild Horse Body 11

Wild Horses in America 12

Habits of Wild Horses 14

Raising Wild Horses 17

The Wild Horse Act 18

Adopting a Wild Horse 20

Glossary 23

Index 24

WILD HORSES

America's wild horses live in the wild, just like deer and antelope. No one takes care of wild horses.

Nearly all of America's wild horses live in the West. There they are free to roam, graze, and raise their babies, or **foals** (FOLZ).

Wild horses look like tame horses. After all, the ancestors of wild horses *were* tame horses.

Wild horses, though, act like wild animals. They are alert and quick to run.

Like mule deer and antelope, the wild horses of the West live in rugged, open country.

WILD HORSE HISTORY

Wild horses are also called **feral** (FER ul) horses. Feral animals are tame animals that live in the wild.

Domestic (duh MES tik), or tame, horses were brought to North America by Spanish explorers about 500 years ago. Later, French and English settlers brought horses to America.

Wild horse herds have been in America since the Spanish brought horses here in the early 1500s.

Most wild horses spend their entire lives in the outdoors—winter, spring, summer, and fall.

Horses became important not only to settlers from Europe, but to Native Americans as well.

Over the centuries, many horses escaped or were released into the wild. They formed herds of wild, or feral, horses.

THE FALL OF WILD HORSES

The herds of wild horses in the American West grew rapidly. By 1900, there may have been 2,000,000 wild horses in the western states.

The horses, though, became a problem, especially to ranchers. Horses graze on many of the same plants as sheep and cattle. Ranchers did not want wild horses eating food needed for their cattle and sheep.

By 1935, most of the wild horses had been shot or sent to slaughterhouses. There they were turned into animal food.

Fearing the loss of cow and sheep food, ranchers killed off wild horses. Wild horses feed on many of the same plants as cattle and sheep.

THE WILD HORSE BODY

Wild horses can be any color that a horse can be—black, gray, brown, white, or some mix of colors.

Wild horses usually stand 14 to 15 **hands** (HANDZ) at the shoulders, or **withers** (WITH erz). Each hand is four inches (ten centimeters), so most wild horses stand about five feet (about one and a half meters) tall.

Wild horses had ancestors from many **breeds** (BREEDZ), or types, of horses. Wild horses often show some of the features of certain ancestors.

Wild horses look like their domestic ancestors.

WILD HORSES IN AMERICA

America's western wild horses are often called mustangs. A few feral horses also live on Chincoteague and Assateague Islands off the coast of Virginia. These are small horses, or ponies. The ponies are probably from Spanish or North African stock. Other breeds, however, have been brought into the herds since the 1920s.

Wild horses of the West are often called mustangs. Some mustangs have the bloodlines of early Spanish horses.

The wild horses of Chincoteague are pony-size.

Most of America's wild horses—some 25,000 of them—live in Nevada. Another 15,000 to 20,000 are spread over Arizona, California, Colorado, Idaho, Montana, New Mexico, Oregon, Utah, and Wyoming. A large private herd lives in South Dakota.

HABITS OF WILD HORSES

Wild horses live in small groups called bands. Most bands are led by a powerful **stallion** (STAL yun), which is a male horse. Younger, weaker stallions form their own bands.

Each spring the herd boss may have to fight other stallions to keep his female horses, or **mares** (MAIRZ).

Like all animals, wild horses need food, water, and shelter. They graze on wild grasses and other plants. They drink from pools and streams. Wild horses find shelter in canyons, valleys, and groves of trees.

Two wild stallions thunder across the cold desert of Nevada.

RAISING WILD HORSES

Most wild horses spend their lives running free and quick as the wind. Several thousand, however, are captured each year and sold to good homes.

New owners usually train their wild horses to be riding mounts. Younger horses train more easily than older ones. Once trained for the saddle, wild horses make tireless, sure-footed riding animals.

Wild horses are especially good in contests that require endurance. Endurance is the ability to do something for a long time.

A wild mare and her foal stand in a holding pen in Palomino Valley near Reno, Nevada. Captured wild horses are sorted here for adoption.

THE WILD HORSE ACT

Wild horses continued to disappear from the United States until 1971. By then, great public concern for their safety led to their protection. The U.S. Congress passed the Wild Free-Roaming Horse and Burro Act.

These cowboys help separate wild horses from captured herds.

Wild horses are rounded up to keep herds in the wild from becoming too large. These young horses are still in shaggy winter coats.

The act is a series of laws. It gave wild horses and **burros** (BUR oz) permanent homes in the West. It also made unlawful any attempt to capture, kill, or even tease wild horses and burros.

The Bureau of Land Management (BLM) took charge of most wild horses and the lands they roam.

ADOPTING A WILD HORSE

To take care of wild horses, the BLM has to be sure that there aren't too many horses for the amount of food they have. Without control, the herds would become huge. Therefore, the BLM captures thousands of horses each year.

The horses are checked by horse doctors and given shots. Then they are put up for adoption at $125 per horse. There are several wild horse adoption centers in the United States. You can write to the BLM (see page 24) for a list.

Wild horses await adoption in Nevada. Hundreds are shipped to adoption centers throughout the U.S.A.

GLOSSARY

breed (BREED) — a particular group of domestic animals having the same characteristics, such as shape or color

burro (BUR o) — a small, wild donkey

domestic (duh MES tik) — a type of animal developed and raised by people to be tame

feral (FER ul) — a domestic animal that has gone to live in the wild

foal (FOL) — a horse before the age of one year

hand (HAND) — a four-inch (ten-centimeter) measure of horses' shoulder height

mare (MAIR) — a mother horse

stallion (STAL yun) — an adult male horse that can father foals

withers (WITH erz) — the ridge between a horse's shoulders

Symbol of America's Old West, wild horses live in a dozen western states.

INDEX

adoption   20

Assateague Island (VA)
   12

breeds   11

Bureau of Land
   Management (BLM)
   19, 20

burros   19

cattle   8

Chincoteague (VA)   12

colors   11

explorer, Spanish   6

foals   5

horses, tame   5, 6

mares   14

mustangs   12

Native Americans   7

ponies   12

ranchers   8

settlers
   English 6
   French 6

sheep   8

stallion   14

West (American)   5, 8

FURTHER READING

Find out more about horses with these helpful books and organizations:
Clutton-Brock, Juliet. *Horse.* Knopf, 1992.
Edwards, Elwyn H. *The Encyclopedia of the Horse.* Dorling Kindersley, Inc., 1994.
Hendricks, Bonnie. *International Encyclopedia of Horse Breeds.* Univ. of Oklahoma, 1995.

Headquarters Office, Bureau of Land Management (BLM), U.S. Dept. of Interior,
   18th and C Streets N.W., Washington, DC 20240-0001
Chincoteague Island Chamber of Commerce, P.O. Box 258, Chincoteague, VA 23336
Southwest Spanish Mustang Registry, 8328 Stevenson Avenue, Sacramento, CA 95828